POETRY Wonderland

Poets From Norfolk & Suffolk

Edited By Megan Roberts

First published in Great Britain in 2019 by:

YoungWriters® Est. 1991

Young Writers
Remus House
Coltsfoot Drive
Peterborough
PE2 9BF
Telephone: 01733 890066
Website: www.youngwriters.co.uk

All Rights Reserved
Book Design by Spencer Hart
© Copyright Contributors 20
SB ISBN 978-1-78988-560-6
Printed and bound in the UK by b
Website: www.bookprintinguk.com
YB0406J

FOREWORD

Here at Young Writers, we love to let imaginations run wild and creativity go crazy. Our aim is to encourage young people to get their creative juices flowing and put pen to paper. Each competition is tailored to the relevant age group, hopefully giving each pupil the inspiration and incentive to create their own piece of creative writing, whether it's a poem or a short story. By allowing them to see their own work in print, we know their confidence and love for the written word will grow.

For our latest competition Poetry Wonderland, we invited primary school pupils to create wild and wonderful poems on any topic they liked – the only limits were the limits of their imagination! Using poetry as their magic wand, these young poets have conjured up worlds, creatures and situations that will amaze and astound or scare and startle! Using a variety of poetic forms of their own choosing, they have allowed us to get a glimpse into their vivid imaginations. We hope you enjoy wandering through the wonders of this book as much as we have.

0.

CONTENTS

Carleton Rode CE (VA) Primary School, Carleton Rode

Lily May Rose (9)	1
Poppy Scarlet Maxey (9)	2
George Kershaw (8)	3
Damien Barrett (7)	4
Jenson Moore (7)	5
Lexi Sophia Smith (8)	6
Amaiah Harrowven (7)	7
Kirsty Payne (8)	8
Zachary Peacock (8)	9

Chelmondiston CE (VC) Primary School, Chelmondiston

Cerys Kitchen (9)	10
Emily Tromans (7)	11
Aliesha Ranson (9)	12
Ashleigh Jane Roberts (9)	13
Freya Donovan (5)	14
Olivia Jefferies (8)	15
Rebekah Jean Findlay (6)	16

Clare Community Primary School, Clare

Tobias Alexander Molton (10)	17
Isla Aim (9)	18
Lanah McIlroy (9)	19
Henrietta Anderson (10)	20
Emily Madden (9)	21
Grae Mileham (10)	22
Ruby Marice Saunders (8)	23
Ira Smith-Adams (9)	24
Logan Terry (9)	25
Sam Hardy (10)	26

Cromer Junior School, Cromer

Ava Sadler (8)	27
Scarlett Keeler (9)	28
Imogen Waplington (9)	30
Kevin Zbigniew Parszcz (8)	31
Kayley Bamford (8)	32
Sophia Yolande Allard (9)	33
Erin Heslin (9)	34
Farrah Girling (9)	35
Amelia Vincent (8)	36
Mina Thalia Fawkes (8)	37
Darcie Minns (8)	38
Logan White (9)	39
Alfie West (9)	40
Blake Branston-Tilley (8)	41
Henri Kew (8)	42
Nathan Broughton (8)	43
Irene Sijo (8)	44
Tommy Wagge (8)	45
Daisy Rose Lunday (9)	46
Iris Moore (8)	47
Scarlett Breeze (8)	48
Ruby Lundie-Nash (8)	49
Leon Perriton (8)	50
Lacey Sanders (9)	51
Kieran Hart (9)	52
Lilia Carey (9)	53
Jack Turner (8)	54
Logan Dawe (8)	55
Bobby Paterson-Bryant (8)	56
Alfie Allum (8)	57
Ethan Cooper (8)	58
Oliver Edward Storey (8)	59

Harry Crayford (8)	60
Reece Keating (8)	61
Charlotte Daniels (8)	62
Jack Boyer (8)	63
Ekaterina Savatova (8)	64
Harvey Breeze (8)	65

Earthsea School, Honingham

Mikey Riley (9)	66
Stevie Weldon (12)	67

Edward Worlledge Ormiston Academy, Great Yarmouth

Dylan Peach (9)	68

Erpingham CE Primary School, Erpingham

Libby Ann Partridge (10)	69
Tilly Hall (10)	70
Jemma Fenton (9)	71

Glebe House School, Hunstanton

Charlie Prout (11)	72
Freddie Gribbin (10)	74
Mabel Crane (11)	76
Eden Hewitt (10)	78
Archie William Rowe (10)	80
Sydney Elizabeth Hipwell (11)	82
Will Saunders (10)	84
Eliza Ann Dix (9)	86
Annabel Lantos (10)	88
Maisie March (10)	90
Scarlett Holly Hallard (10)	91
Emelia King (10)	92
Orla Emily Haslam (10)	94
Gracie-Mae Elizabeth Meek (10)	95
Giovanni Giubileo (10)	96
Jonny Goode (10)	97
Edward Gostling (9)	98
Emily Kilby (10)	99
Ferdi Macewan (10)	100

Philippa Hingley (7)	101
Harry Jack John Hammond (9)	102

Great Dunham Primary School, Great Dunham

Freya Whitlock (9)	103
William Gardam (7)	104
Lyra Hill (9)	106
Gracie Garner (9)	108
Archie Cook (7)	109
Bella Hill (7)	110
Holly Jessica Susan Appleby (7)	111
Betha Chantry (9)	112
Esme Moxey (8)	113
Max Prochazka (8)	114
Jessica Wild (9)	115
Jamie White (7)	116
Isobel Clifton (9)	117
William Thomas Cooper (8)	118

Great Heath Academy, Mildenhall

Laurence Redman (7)	119
Sola Akindiji (7)	120
Hayley Matzk (8)	121
Clervi Kemp (8)	122
Khloe Davidson (7)	123

Hevingham Primary School, Hevingham

Jaimee Andrews (9)	124
Marian Jane Sinclair-Russell (9)	125

Hockering CE (VC) Primary School, Hockering

Maisey Reading (7)	126
Melody-Maye Birch-Rodney (7)	128
Tallulah Kati Goodwin (10)	129
Dorothy Iwo (9)	130

St Helen's Primary School, Ipswich

Chester Joscelyne (10)	131
Viktorija Gerlikaite (10)	132
Bonnie Elvin (10)	134
Callum Matthew Papworth (11)	136
Ollie Joseph (11)	138
Asal Azhdari (10)	140
Jonah George Merchant (10)	142
Amelia Grzesiak (10)	144
Nathan Watson (8)	146
Scarlett Borrett (9)	148
Evie Armstrong (10)	150
Nicholas Mikov (10)	151
Alfred Catherall (10)	152
Emily Yeung (10)	153
Esme Ellen Merchant (8)	154
Tahiya Afsana Hye (9)	155
Yosr Al Hassan (11)	156
Tess Thompson (9)	157
Alfie Weston (10)	158
Cooper Flurrie (7)	159
Malik Nour (7)	160

St Margaret's Primary Academy, Lowestoft

Olivia Ali (7)	161
Tess Smith (10)	162
Jodi-Mae Leaper (9)	163
Lilli Smith-Cushion (9)	164
Imogen Louise Lungenmuss-Ward (9)	165
Taio Xavier Dyer (8)	166
Gracey Leitch (7)	167
Connor-Joe Reeve (8)	168
Malaja White (7)	169
Kaitlyn Rihanna (9)	170
Brayden Finnigan	171
Lexie-Mai Finnigan (7)	172
Ava Cregan (7)	173
Ellie Davies (8)	174
Imogen Ardley (7)	175
Liam Coote (7)	176
Megan Hammond (9)	177
Adi Shuckford (10)	178
Serena Summer Ruby Goulbourne (9)	179
Savannah Georgina Gail Wild (8)	180
Eve-Louise Chapman (8)	181
Mary-Jane Joyce Gammage (8)	182
Liam Gee (9)	183
Aidan Green (9)	184

The Poems

My Swimming Pool

When I said 'swimming pool'
I didn't exactly mean a swimming pool...

I just wanted some food
I said that I wanted a swimming pool as well

But, well, my brother filled the room with water
Not exactly what I wanted

When I arrived, I fell in
My clothes turned into a bikini

The mermaids greeted me
With great kindness

They helped me choose the perfect tail
I bought a merpet too

When I dived down, I heard the mermaids singing
I saw the mermaids swimming with their merpets

And finally, I found some food
It was hidden right at the bottom!

Lily May Rose (9)
Carleton Rode CE (VA) Primary School, Carleton Rode

The Kitten That Lived In A Mushroom

There was a kitten and his name was Mittens
He lived in a red and white mushroom
All cosy and warm
And he loved his bed
He'd sleep in it from evening to dawn
He heard a quiet breeze
Felt the soft floor
Mice liked to hide under his squeaky door
In his cold, icy fridge
Was fish and mushroom stew
And his favourite drink was milk
From his cow, Moo Moo
In his room, there were dolls
And if you were hungry
You could take a bite out of the mushroom walls.

Poppy Scarlet Maxey (9)
Carleton Rode CE (VA) Primary School, Carleton Rode

Inside Out

One day, I woke up and I was inside someone
My feet were squelchy welchy
I could hear his heart beating
The bones were crunchy munchy
I was riding through the blood vessels
The food was smelly welly
My feet were sinking in
My fingers were freezing
My clothes were soggy woggy
One day, the man coughed
And I came flying out
I came straight out of his mouth!

George Kershaw (8)
Carleton Rode CE (VA) Primary School, Carleton Rode

Burger Moon City

I got there in a ketchup bottle
I went up to space
I went to Burger Moon City
The roll was bouncy
The seeds were hard
The ketchup was sloppy
The cheese was all melted
The chips were floating around
The lettuce was crunchy
The onions were stinky
What a strange moon it was!

Damien Barrett (7)
Carleton Rode CE (VA) Primary School, Carleton Rode

Jumping On Clouds

I jumped on clouds
And I saw Cake Land
It was bouncy
And very crumbly
The icing was squishy
The marshmallow trees were sticky
My feet were covered in icing
The houses were made out of cake
What a wonderful day I had!
I hope I'm not completely mad!

Jenson Moore (7)
Carleton Rode CE (VA) Primary School, Carleton Rode

Candy World

I arrived in a candy world
There was a chocolate path
There were lollipops for trees
There were unicorns all around
There was a chocolate house
The grass was made of marshmallow bits
It was sticky, very sticky
This strange candy world.

Lexi Sophia Smith (8)
Carleton Rode CE (VA) Primary School, Carleton Rode

Jello House

When I got back from school
I opened the jello door
I screamed out loud, "It's jello!"
I can't believe my house changed
My mum told me to take my shoes off outside
Then I bounced away
In my new jello house.

Amaiah Harrowven (7)
Carleton Rode CE (VA) Primary School, Carleton Rode

Cookie Moon

I arrived in space
In a fire-boosted car
To my surprise, there were sea creatures up there!
There were so many chocolate chips
The moon was a cookie
It was rock hard
I almost fell off the edge of this weird, flat moon!

Kirsty Payne (8)
Carleton Rode CE (VA) Primary School, Carleton Rode

DJ Mello

I was in a marshmallow disco
My whole body was vibrating
I saw marshmallows all around me
I got invited to be a DJ
I played some great tunes
People wanted my autograph
And I DJed all night long.

Zachary Peacock (8)
Carleton Rode CE (VA) Primary School, Carleton Rode

The Elf That Came For Tea

A happy elf came for tea
He was really excited and full of glee
As I asked him if he wanted a cup of tea
He said, "No thanks," while swinging around
Like a monkey in a tree
I sat down while he said to me
"Do not whine or I'll put you upside down."
"You're as funny as a clown."
I cheered up a bit
So I thought I should dangle upside down
When the elf left, I was really happy and full of glee
I asked him, "Next time, can I go to yours for tea?"

Cerys Kitchen (9)
Chelmondiston CE (VC) Primary School, Chelmondiston

The Walking, Talking, Seeing Door Handle

T he walking, talking, seeing door handle
H e is shiny and gold
E very time I see him, it's fun

D ream of how we always play
O pen the door and see him twice
O pen your mouth and say hello
R ound and round we go!

H ave a wonderful time together
A mazing friends forever
N ow I have to go
D o hope we see each other again
L ying in my den
E veryone will never know.

Emily Tromans (7)
Chelmondiston CE (VC) Primary School, Chelmondiston

Strange Love

S trange love is when a
T -rex falls completely
R andomly in love
A doring, addicted and
N ever going to stop loving a
G riffin!
E veryone looks and stares

L aughing at their strange love
O bviously jealous, but everyone knows the
V ictorious, strange couple are
E xtremely in love!

Aliesha Ranson (9)
Chelmondiston CE (VC) Primary School, Chelmondiston

I Am A Puddle

I am a puddle, created by the rain
The sun is my enemy
The heat is such a pain

In winter, you can splash in me
Only if you wear wellies
'Cause socks and shoes I will make damp
And very, very smelly
If it freezes overnight
I will become ice and slippery
So enjoy me while you can
But only dogs can safely drink me.

Ashleigh Jane Roberts (9)
Chelmondiston CE (VC) Primary School, Chelmondiston

Cat Kingdom

Cat king sits on the throne
Cat queen goes shopping for milk
Cat prince plays with a mouse
Cat princess gets ready for school
Cat choir sings with loud meows
Cat farmer chases the cows
Cat doctor cuts some claws
Cat vet puts bandages on paws
Cat chef cooks a feast of fish
Cats with full bellies sleep and sleep.

Freya Donovan (5)
Chelmondiston CE (VC) Primary School, Chelmondiston

Animals Running Free!

Horses running around, like thunder and lightning
Pigs rolling about in mud, like crazy people
Sheep so woolly I could die
Goats' horns so sharp, like a knife
Cows' milk so tasty, like fairy dust rushing through your body
Donkeys so soft, like a fluffy teddy bear.

Olivia Jefferies (8)
Chelmondiston CE (VC) Primary School, Chelmondiston

The Funny Jungle

There are funny animals out and about
Some in the jungle and some have sneaked out
The monkeys slide down the rainbows
Elephants are being groomed from head to toe
But the Zeonkephant stays in the jungle
All on its own.

Rebekah Jean Findlay (6)
Chelmondiston CE (VC) Primary School, Chelmondiston

Rexy

Far, far away, way beyond the sun
Was the Isle of Rex, where dinosaurs would run
There lived a dinosaur, Rexy was his name
He wasn't like the other dinosaurs as he was lame
Rexy just loved to dance and prance and sing
Boogieing in his pink tutu was his favourite thing
He auditioned for a talent show (he wasn't very good)
All the other dinosaurs laughed because no one understood
But Rexy didn't care, he just wanted to have fun
After all, what was so special about being able to run?

Tobias Alexander Molton (10)
Clare Community Primary School, Clare

The Lovely Midsummer

The pig lay on the sweet-smelling grass
With the sound of bees and butterflies filling the air
And the brook bubbled and gurgled around the bend
The cotton wool clouds floated by
Amongst the noise came a terrible sound
That made the pig remove his sunglasses
And stand his ground
For there in the sky was a sight to be seen
A long-eared bunnycopter
Dropping popcorn everywhere
Being driven by a ladybird in a fancy chair!

Isla Aim (9)
Clare Community Primary School, Clare

Getting Home For Tea

Getting home for tea
Was a challenge for me
And my two pets
Dogfrog and Dragon
We were playing ball
When Mum gave the call
But a submarine
Was blocking our path
And Dogfrog started to howl
Dogfrog hopped from side to side
And barked at the top of his voice
While Dragon puffed smoke
In his face
The driver couldn't see
Due to the manic confusion
And we all got back for tea.

Lanah McIlroy (9)
Clare Community Primary School, Clare

The Craziest Birthday Ever!

Today is my tenth birthday
And I'm having a party
Not just any party though
My party is in space!
I've got loads planned
We're going to play crater-jumping
Pass the moon rock
Ride the shooting star
Pin the tail on the alien
And... guess what?
We're getting there by rocket!
I have a feeling that today
Will be the craziest birthday ever!

Henrietta Anderson (10)
Clare Community Primary School, Clare

The Dog On Roller Skates

The dog slides by on his skates
He's gliding on the cold wood
His fur is going behind him while he glides
His legs are tumbling down and out
He is getting very tired
With his tongue hanging out
He really needs a drink
He slips and slides to his mother
All the people stare at him
While he drinks his water
It is time to go home.

Emily Madden (9)
Clare Community Primary School, Clare

Diving Deep

Diver, diver
Diving deep
Diving through the coral reef
Up and down, round and round
Through the shimmery water

Diver, diver
Diving deep
Diving through blue waters so sleek

Diver, diver
Diving deep
Diving through coral sleek

Diver, diver
Diving deep
Diving through squids' ink.

Grae Mileham (10)
Clare Community Primary School, Clare

The Unicorn

One day, I met a unicorn
She was very white
When the sun shone on her
Her coat glowed so bright

I named her Candy
Because she was so sweet
She would dance
On her little feet.

But one day
She had to go
Back to where the unicorns
Played in the deep, white snow.

Ruby Marice Saunders (8)
Clare Community Primary School, Clare

The Clumsiest Day Of My Life

Today I smooched a shark
Who barked while in a bath
And after my bath
I danced with a giraffe
Who gave a ride to a baboon
As they sunbathed on the moon

Although my day was good
I got prickles in my foot
While hugging a cow
I did a lovely bow.

Ira Smith-Adams (9)
Clare Community Primary School, Clare

An Elf Came To Swim With Me

An elf came from Santa
To deliver my presents
But stayed instead
To swim with me
The elf was named Buddy
And he liked to play around
We swam up and dived down
Until night fell
Then we drank hot chocolate
And he went back to the North Pole.

Logan Terry (9)
Clare Community Primary School, Clare

The Dog And The Football

The dog and the football
They jumped through the goal
Up to space
Saw an astronaut
Went to the moon
Ran on Uranus
Went into a black hole
Into another universe
The ball popped on a cactus
And the dog ran away to a cave.

Sam Hardy (10)
Clare Community Primary School, Clare

Doggy Went For A Walk

There once was a dog
Who was tired of a log
That sat in a bog next door
So he settled down
And told himself, "What if I go and explore?"
So he took a walk down the village
And all he saw was a bucket of water
So he tried the lake around the corner
The next thing he knew, there was a vast doughnut
That sat in front of him
So he jumped onto it
And he went down the river
After a while, they reached a waterfall
But then he looked around and saw a sweetie world
But before he fell, he jumped on a piece of liquorice
Then he sat on a candy swing
He was lost, then he fell
But he fell onto a trampoline in his garden
But he was home.

Ava Sadler (8)
Cromer Junior School, Cromer

Icklewoo

There was once a dog called Icklewoo
I wondered why he wore two shoes
He looked kind of strange
Fluffy and orange and yellow-striped too
And he sat on a flying cloud of candyfloss
In the daytime, continuously shouting, "Yahoo!"
And when it was night, he wrapped himself
In a massive sock and sat in a shoe
Yes, a shoe
Not something you see every day
He also liked eating sweet, sticky honey
When I woke up, I stared in shock
I couldn't see the sock that he liked to hang on the wall
Which was about nine feet tall
I could not believe that he had ripped down the trees
Honey was dripping from peas in the fridge
Whoosh! "What's that?" I cried, terrified
Then the creature said, "It's me, Icklewoo,
You know, the one who was flying in a shoe."

"Oh, I'm sorry, I should have known it was you, Icklewoo, the one who flies in a shoe," I giggled.

Scarlett Keeler (9)
Cromer Junior School, Cromer

The Mouse Who Found Out The Moon Wasn't Cheese

T here was a mouse who lived on the moon
H e thought the moon was made of cheese
E very day of his life, he wanted to eat the moon.

"M ouse, what if the moon isn't cheese?
O h no! He doesn't know that the moon isn't cheese!"
O n the mouse was a spacesuit
N o one knew the mouse lived on the moon.

M ouse was just about to take a bite out of the moon
O n the moon was a star that landed behind him
U nder him, a crack appeared
"S tar, fly away so I can eat the moon!"
E ventually, Mouse found out that the moon wasn't made of cheese.

Imogen Waplington (9)
Cromer Junior School, Cromer

The Candyland Dream

I woke up and went outside
N ever remembered this

C andy was everywhere and the smell had changed
A nd it was colourful
N ever saw this
D igging underground into icing
Y ep, this never happened
L ittle icing balls ready to make
A nd everlasting candyfloss clouds crumbling all around
N ever feared the ocean as it was apple juice
D reaming was really enjoyable

A nd then I woke up in my normal world
F reedom from my crazy dream
T hen I found I was trapped
E nding my dream
"R ip the paper," I said to myself.

Kevin Zbigniew Parszcz (8)
Cromer Junior School, Cromer

Space Crazy Fun

Once in a dream, something crazy happened
I saw a green zebra that was randomly patterned
Nearby, there was a black belt dolphin
They were both sleeping in deep slumber
Were they having a party and would they have cucumber?
If they were, that would be good
Maybe, if they were lucky, they would have their own pool
The friends had just met something funny
But it didn't like honey
The new friend liked to sing and dance
He was a hot dog and he wore a suit
The three friends did not prance
Instead, they found an acorn
The four friends went to space
And that's where they are today.

Kayley Bamford (8)
Cromer Junior School, Cromer

The Goblin Who Froze In Ice

There was once a goblin who lived in a bog
He got bored with a log
He sat down on a log, set off down the river
Later on, he found himself rushing down a waterfall
And landed with a thump!
He thought to himself, *I want to go ice skating*
So he made some skates out of a tree
And the tree was made out of Kit Kats
But the goblin didn't know that
So he found the ice rink and the Kit Kat skates froze
So his feet froze to the skates and he was stuck
Then he started getting hungry
So he started munching on his skates
But he was still stuck because
He was frozen from the cold.

Sophia Yolande Allard (9)
Cromer Junior School, Cromer

Cotton Candy Cutie Land

Unicorns sleep on cotton candy beds
They sit on candy chairs
Also, they swim in laces
And don't like seeing bears
If they see a bear
They will turn into a pear
They sleep like crazy
So don't be crazy
Otherwise, you will be lazy
You can eat your bed
But don't eat the teddy, Ted
Otherwise, something will hurt
Like your belly
So don't do anything on this list
Because you will meet Mr Hiss
Mr Hiss goes like this: sss
So don't meet him or Mrs Hiss
Cotton candy is the best, so
Just take loads of rest in a nest.

Erin Heslin (9)
Cromer Junior School, Cromer

The Adventures Of Mr P Cake And Me!

Me and Mr P Cake got into a rocket
And then he slid me into his pocket
Then I started to shout, "Mr P Cake, let's make a song!"
We laughed and did it 'til we arrived in Hong Kong
We played and swam too
Then Mr P Cake needed the loo
Me and Mr P Cake got into the rocket
And, yet again, I got into his pocket
We zoomed back home and I rode on his back
Along the butter and syrup river
Then we got home and I started to shiver
But it was okay, he turned on the heat
The day was over so I got into bed, under the sheet!

Farrah Girling (9)
Cromer Junior School, Cromer

The Lemon Hide-And-Seek

I was playing hide-and-seek with a lemon
We played it from midnight to midday in the fridge
I hid behind a pip
I was sneaking behind the seeker
But juice squirted into my eyes
It started to rain candyfloss
It helped, but I got stuck
I couldn't move out of the way
Until... *Squish!*
Onto a fish
I escaped
But I got caught in a Loom band
A dog-kingfisher called Spot helped me
I took her for a trot
Me and my friends saw her newborn puppies
They were all sisters.

Amelia Vincent (8)
Cromer Junior School, Cromer

Pink Bananas

Pink bananas everywhere
Dancing to the beat
Disco globes high
Balloons are going to the moon
In Balloon Village, everything's fun
All the bananas are playing games
It's hard not to pop the balloons
With all the bananas' pointy tips
Pink bananas everywhere
Jumping up and down
Pink balloons tripping up
Falling to the ground
Every banana hurt their leg
Dancing round and round
All bananas on the ground
All bananas on top of the ground.

Mina Thalia Fawkes (8)
Cromer Junior School, Cromer

Aleesha In Wonderland!

There once was a girl called Aleesha
She fell into a deep sleep
Her dream was to be in Wonderland
Every single thing was talking
The trees replied, "It's okay, we're all friendly."
"That's okay then, I thought
You were going to eat me!" replied Aleesha
"Don't you worry, we would never do that
To you, even though we are hungry," said the tree
She then woke up and said, "Ow! It was a dream."

Darcie Minns (8)
Cromer Junior School, Cromer

Monster Trouble

The monster ate my food
He slept in my bed
He ate my couch
He ate my dad
He ate my mum
He ate all of my pets
"Gosh, what a hungry monster!" I screeched
Then he ate my comics
He chewed my Lego into tiny pieces
He ate my bed
And he ate me
Gosh, what a lot he ate today
"I wish he didn't eat me at all
Because I'm his best friend," I shouted
Then he ate my house
Then he ate the whole world!

Logan White (9)
Cromer Junior School, Cromer

My Trip To The Beach

My trip to the beach was weird...

The beach ball net was broken
A dinosaur ate my picnic
He kicked my ball away
His breath ruined the beach break
My blanket got stuck
The dinosaur stepped on it
He buried me in seashells
He ate a fish, he ate a fish
He ate a pirate
But I couldn't see
He sat on me
Then he ran wild
Waving his t-shirt
Hang on, it was just my brother
Wearing a costume.

Alfie West (9)
Cromer Junior School, Cromer

The Running Moon

T he moon was running
H e didn't stop unless he fell
E very time he ran, he was good.

M oving to the ends, he still ran
O ver the track, he looked to see
O ne of the biggest rings. He got
N ear it, he got it and floated up.

R unning to the end to win
A nd if he got there, he would get a golden
N yan Cat. He finally got there, but he was second.

Blake Branston-Tilley (8)
Cromer Junior School, Cromer

A Dragon Farting Out Meatballs And Chocolate Balls

The dragon flew above the clouds
Farting meatballs out of its bum
Burning the trees with its fire-breathing mouth
Moving side to side, up and down
Dodging all the green trees in its way
Flapping its wings, head to toe
Balls falling from clouds
Hitting the fire-breathing dragon
Smashing the dragon's wings
Making the dragon fart out chocolate balls
Burping out hot candy cane sticks. Ouch!

Henri Kew (8)
Cromer Junior School, Cromer

Cookie Monster's Lair

Jump down the hole
You smile with glee
Down, down, down
Fall so deep
All you see is cookies
A cookie stuffs his face
You tried to hide, but it's too late
He wants to eat you too
There you sit, eating cookies
Then you ask, "Can I go?"
"Yes, follow me."
Down a deep, dark tunnel he goes
"Now go," he says
"Come back tomorrow."

Nathan Broughton (8)
Cromer Junior School, Cromer

Pink Fluffy Unicorns

I saw pink, fluffy unicorns
I saw a rainbow in the sky
It was so high above me
In the distance, a rainbow shot
From a yellow-orange bum
It had some rainbow on it too
I tried to catch it with my hand
It flew away into the pink clouds
Zooming into the sun above
With its horn pointing up
I had fun with it for some time
Until it flew to Wonderland.

Irene Sijo (8)
Cromer Junior School, Cromer

Flying With A Baby

Oh no! The baby's nappy fell off
And it's right in my face!
He's eaten all the tasty stuff
And left the yucky stuff for me!
At least I have some drinks to fill me up
He's drunk them too! Oh, what will I do?
There's still some milk left
Now, I've lost him, where did he go?
Come back! I don't want
To be told off by your mum!

Tommy Wagge (8)
Cromer Junior School, Cromer

Transforming

T he land where people transform
R ules are banned
A lso, lots of different types
N one of them are normal
S piders playing guitars
F ollow their dreams
O ne colourful cookie
R unning rhinos
M illions of unicorns playing
I n a dream
N o limits
G oblins are even alive!

Daisy Rose Lunday (9)
Cromer Junior School, Cromer

The Candy Dragon

I fell down a rabbit hole and I saw
A dragon made out of candy
It had candy cane-patterned skin
Hair made out of candyfloss
Eyes that looked like curly lollipops
He also had rock candy shapes on his back
But the thing that was really horrible was
The candy dragon pooped buttons
After that, I said that I was going to call him
Buttons.

Iris Moore (8)
Cromer Junior School, Cromer

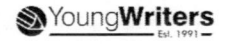

Candy Cats

I found a land of colourful lollipops
I thought I saw a cat
I thought it was my imagination
But I saw it again
I jumped in and saw a cat covered in lollipops
All of the cat's friends came alone
They brought the lollipop king
And he gave me a lollipop crown
And became my friend
So I bought a sweet biscuit.

Scarlett Breeze (8)
Cromer Junior School, Cromer

Monsters Flossing On Ice

In an ice wonderland, monsters floss
People walk by and think, *how weird*
People throw up while the monsters dribble
Because how gross would that be
If people started to dribble?
Monsters floss all day on the ice while they tumble
Because they're clumsy and colourful, just like clowns.

Ruby Lundie-Nash (8)
Cromer Junior School, Cromer

Black Hole

B eing sucked into the black hole
L ightning in the black hole
A ir making me cough
C loser, closer, closer!
K eep getting closer

H ow am I going to escape?
O h no
L anding signals breaking up
E rror, error, error.

Leon Perriton (8)
Cromer Junior School, Cromer

Underground Party

The skeletons were having a disco
As the pelicans were eating their seeds
Underground or in the sky
They all wanted to fly

All the dead were dancing
As all the birds were prancing
The noise was very loud
The people were really proud
So happy, they were chanting.

Lacey Sanders (9)
Cromer Junior School, Cromer

Food Disaster

I wake up and I can see
A chocolate volcano!
I ride a fish finger
There is tomato sauce everywhere
I realise- "Argh!" I'm in Food Land!
My friend, Kevin, is swimming
In a tsunami made out of icing
It's raining tacos and
There's a bread earthquake.

Kieran Hart (9)
Cromer Junior School, Cromer

Over The Clouds

Cats flapping their wings
Soaring above the trees
Singing to trees below
Wings flapping gracefully
Eyes shimmering in the sky
Going through rainbows
Turning tiny, then big, tiny, then big
Orange sky
Clouds freeze, blowing cats
Flowers rising to giant size!

Lilia Carey (9)
Cromer Junior School, Cromer

Danger, Danger Dinosaur

D anger, danger
I n came a dinosaur into McDonald's
N o one liked him
O rdered chips
S moothie, a cheeseburger
A nd a T-rex toy
U nder the dinosaur was the counter
"R oar!" said the dinosaur.

Jack Turner (8)
Cromer Junior School, Cromer

Everything's In Space

I see Santa dabbing in space
I see a cookie and a burger planet
I see trees and gremlins on mushrooms
I see pirate ships like spaceships
I see money floating and dinosaurs playing guitars
I see dragons brushing their teeth
I see elves farting in space.

Logan Dawe (8)
Cromer Junior School, Cromer

The Running Hedgehog

One day, a hedgehog was running on the moon
He found a lair
He decided to go inside
Inside was dusty and there were spiders
And rusty, metal stairs leading down
To a cell full of skeletons
He got scared and ran out
And never came back.

Bobby Paterson-Bryant (8)
Cromer Junior School, Cromer

My Pie Up High

My pie up high, hey, that was my pie. "Hi!"
My pie up high, smelly and white at night
My pie up high was eaten by a fly
My pie up high, way up in the sky
My pie up high, smelling in the sky
My pie up high, I found a goblin in my pie.

Alfie Allum (8)
Cromer Junior School, Cromer

The Attack Of The Watermelon Beast

A watermelon was eating everyone
He ate my brother, who was also candy
Under attack and nothing to do
But send the gummy soldiers to war
But *gulp!* Down they went into the watermelon's tummy
We just had the gulp left...

Ethan Cooper (8)
Cromer Junior School, Cromer

The Rhinos

On a football pitch
My team was beaten by a team of rhinos
A player was butted into space
By the pointed rhino horn
The goalkeeper was trampled
As flat as a pancake
Before almost everyone
We ended the match!

Oliver Edward Storey (8)
Cromer Junior School, Cromer

Pig Time

P eculiar pig on the beach
I t is not very nice
G reat, I'm soaked!

T ime to go home
I n the car
M aybe that's good enough
E agerly excited to go to bed.

Harry Crayford (8)
Cromer Junior School, Cromer

Nonsense Land

Tiny giraffes laughing
Blue elephants singing
Purple sharks swinging in the trees
Rainbow dragons wearing glasses
Red spider eating a carrot
A submarine driving from shop to shop
Stickmen dancing in a tree.

Reece Keating (8)
Cromer Junior School, Cromer

The Candy Land In The Sky!

In a land far away in the sky
A dragon was eating, I wonder why?
And fancy that, he was with the queen
Eating tasty chocolate ice cream
The other side of this wonderful land
Was covered with fizzy, sherbet sand!

Charlotte Daniels (8)
Cromer Junior School, Cromer

Super Dog

Super Dog was the best
Unordinary he was
But he was perfect for
Saving cities from Cat Man
Rush City was under attack!
"Darn! Cat Man has gone!
Oh no! My mask!
My secret identity is gone!"

Jack Boyer (8)
Cromer Junior School, Cromer

Springtime

The fruits danced
The breeze sprinted
The leaves on the trees drifted
Mushrooms swung from side to side
In the breeze, like a big, popping sneeze
The mushrooms were scared
The leaves were aware.

Ekaterina Savatova (8)
Cromer Junior School, Cromer

Chocolate Volcano

The volcano rumbled like a crazy machine
Shooting chocolate out of the top
Bang! Like a firework
Chocolate running down the side
Puddles of delicious, runny chocolate
Mmm...

Harvey Breeze (8)
Cromer Junior School, Cromer

The Cookie Land

The picnic is over
The cookies are soggy
Vinegary
Sugary
Too much toffee
Too creamy
And I can't see because the crazy cookie monster is eating me.

Mikey Riley (9)
Earthsea School, Honingham

Stevie's Phone

Stevie likes iPhones
Not Samsung
Or Binatone
But an iPhone
Not a Motorola
Or a flip phone
But a brilliant iPhone.

Stevie Weldon (12)
Earthsea School, Honingham

Mad Tea Party

Today I'll go to a tea party
It'll be lots of fun
We'll spin around and play some games
And the fun will have just begun

We dance around like crazy
Tea is everywhere
The cups smell like a daisy
We all jump in the air.

Cups are stacked high everywhere
Everyone eats with such greed
When the cakes come out, everyone will stare
And say, "Thanks," because he has done a great deed.

Dylan Peach (9)
Edward Worlledge Ormiston Academy, Great Yarmouth

The Girl Of Crazy Colours

Dream far away and you will meet
A girl upon a different street
Where colours move a different way
And the sky is never grey
Listen hard and you will hear
A girl of crazy colours near.

Scarlet green ribbons run through
Her golden red hair
Which lies over her kingfisher-blue face
Her tangy orange, violet knees bend
So her smoky-white fingertips
Can touch her indigo yellow toes
Her sky-blue, pink nose crinkles
As neon grey eyes stare out at you
Then within a moment, she is gone
Leaving a trail of emerald purple
Footsteps behind her.

Have you ever seen this girl?
Well, if you search where your dreams hide
You will find her right inside.

Libby Ann Partridge (10)
Erpingham CE Primary School, Erpingham

The Wobble Wacky

It was a moggy day and the wobble was wobbling
The struthious beast wobbled in the wacky river
All he had in his tummy was honey
Then he realised he had paws, not claws
He saw a fish on a dish and went to dive in
But then he heard a din
Then he saw a band of ants
That were playing the drums
The drums were made from a dragon's shoe
And the grass was as green as Grandad's kazoo.

Tilly Hall (10)
Erpingham CE Primary School, Erpingham

Violent Volcano

V iolent crashes and bangs
O uter core heats the magma
L oading plumes of lava splash
C alling birds to fly and die
A nimals run but are trapped in the forest
N ow the forest is black and white
O ut of the lava.

Jemma Fenton (9)
Erpingham CE Primary School, Erpingham

Red Bull Shark Soapbox Race

I never thought I'd see
A soapbox race under the sea!

First to go past was the sardine tin piloted by...
You guessed it! Sardines
Talk about a crowded ride
More like a silvery, swirling shoal!
The driver couldn't see
And they crashed on the final bend.

Next up was the hermit crab
With 'go faster' stripes on his shell
The starting pistol went and he was off
But going sideways? Was that allowed?
He didn't exactly make a decent time
But it was good to watch.

Here was Sid Skate, lining up his skateboard
What a rad ray! Shades on and really to roll
Tricks and stunts all the way down the course
And the crowd loved it!

He nearly broke the course record
But it was still held by a flying fish from 2015.

Here came the clownfish in their anemone car
Tentacles whirling, wow, what a speed!
Surely they would win
But on the final bump
They got the angle wrong and spun into a reef.

Finally, an octopus on a tandem
Now I've seen it all
Six tentacles peddling like mad
And two on the handlebars
And changing colour on every twist and turn
By the end, he was bright red from the effort
But it was worth it as he flew into joint first with Sid.

Charlie Prout (11)
Glebe House School, Hunstanton

The Dragon That Joined Our School

Today was the day the dragon joined our class
He was great and tall and called Jeffery
And had bright red skin with dazzling green eyes.

At first break, it didn't go well
Jeffery could not fit through the astrogate
Then he went to the football pitch
And surprisingly, he was great.

When it got to lunch, it was a problem
He wanted to eat all the food
When it came to sitting down
He had to use a whole bench!

Jeffery did not have a great first day
But as the year continued, he got better
He won the most sports awards ever.

In the holidays, he had some friends visit
All the friends said his house was huge
What was even more amazingly spectacular were his pets

He had a crocodile, a cheetah, a lion, an orangutan and a chameleon.

There was a brand new camping night
That Jeffery signed up to
During the night, there was a fire-lighting contest
And of course, Jeffery won.

It was finally the summer holidays
And of course, Jeffery went on holiday
He just got up and flew to that place.

During the summer holidays, he had grown a lot
And everyone was shocked and surprised
But he had now settled in fully
And was ready for another year.

Freddie Gribbin (10)
Glebe House School, Hunstanton

My Dad Is A Ballet Dancer!

I woke up as the clock struck midnight
I heard a faint sound of music floating in the air
"What could this be?" I said
So I got out of bed to investigate

I crept down the stairs
And tiptoed down the hallway
I threw on my coat, hat and gloves
And I went outside to find out more

I walked to the garage as quiet as a mouse
I heard the pitter-patter of feet on the floor
So I looked through the keyhole and saw
My dad was doing ballet!

My big, hairy, mechanic dad
Who can't even clap in time
Was dancing around the floor in a tutu
As light as a Sugar Puff

As prettily as a fairy, he did a graceful pirouette

Plié, arabesque, jeté, all a breeze
Spinning around and twirling like water down a plughole
And leaping through the air like a gazelle

Then the music stopped
He was out of breath and I was speechless
Then he started to walk towards the door
I ran as fast as my legs could carry me to my room

I woke up the next morning, was it all a dream?
I raced to the garage and looked around
His toolbox drawer was slightly ajar
I saw a gleam of pink satin peeking out the crack

My dad is a ballet dancer!

Mabel Crane (11)
Glebe House School, Hunstanton

All Thanks To That One Chest In The Snow

I step outside and see the lovely, snowy scene
There seems to be a chest
What on earth could it be?
I put my hand in and get pulled away
"Argh!"
Is that the moon made out of cheese?
What on earth could it be?
I reach the end of the chest, this is such a mess!
A bird, a line, a bee? What on earth could it be?
A mushroom and a lollipop mixed into one
This is such a dream!
The white rabbit, seven feet tall
What on earth could it be?
There's a dragon mixed with a dog called Dan
What on earth could it be?
There's a door with a key
What on earth could it be?
Put the key in and what could it be?
A tree? A tree? It looks like a tree

Is it candyfloss or a bee, branches or these?
Climb up the tree, what could it be?
A rocket? A dragon? A key and me
But what is that I see?
Is it a house or a tree? What on earth could it be?
Walk closer and closer and what do I see?
A house, a house, made just for me
I love it, I love it and what is that I see?
A dragon! Aww, he is so cute, even more than a bee
I will live here forever and ever
Even more than he
And all thanks to that one chest
In the snowy scene.

Eden Hewitt (10)
Glebe House School, Hunstanton

Living In The Insect Kingdom

There was once a little boy called Archie
Who always wondered what it would be like
In the jungle with the insects
He thought and thought until he was desperate
Finally, a few days later, his wish came true!

He woke up to find himself in the insect kingdom
He got out of bed and ventured into the trees
Loads of insects, not small but huge!
Archie was in the middle of the jungle!

The first thing he saw was the ants' nest
And I mean big, huge, great things
Big as boulders, maybe even bigger
The animals were just simply, simply amazing
So he adventured some more.

Just then, he saw a giant spider. Luckily, Archie liked spiders
The spider had an egg sac as big as a chair
And Archie approached it and touched it

The baby spiders poured out like yolk
Falling out of an egg onto toast.

Just then, he awoke to find himself at home
He figured out it was just a dream
He was kind of upset that his adventure was over
He knew, until next time, that was the end.

Archie William Rowe (10)
Glebe House School, Hunstanton

Underneath

Can you imagine underneath the ocean?
Underneath the sky and the sea and the sand?

There is a land no one can go to
A city of emeralds
Cut off from the world

You can hear the soft bells
That chime from the church tower
You can hear the birds
That sing from the trees

Everything is covered with a carpet of green
A carpet of algae
Not showing a sign
Of where you have been

The buildings themselves are so different from here
Nooks and crannies everywhere
They stand tall but are about to collapse
They have been here since time elapsed

There is a shipwreck that came from afar
Lost and gone, off the radar

The treasure they collected
Is hiding down there
Probably hidden in the captain's great lair

This city stands tall
And the spirits all sing
Their voices not talking
Their voices all ring

Come and see this land
Somewhere from afar
Where the city stands tall
And where the spirits are.

Sydney Elizabeth Hipwell (11)
Glebe House School, Hunstanton

My Trip To The Moon Goes Wrong!

It was all going so well
My spaceship had started for the first time
My packed lunch was my favourite pasta
As we flew up in the sky

As we approached the moon
Something seemed very strange
The spaceship smelled like breakfast
And started to get warm

I looked out of the window
And saw that the moon's surface was bubbling away
It did not look like cheese at all
And it certainly wasn't rock!

I lowered the spaceship down
Slurp!
We sank down into the surface
Slowly sinking and slurping downwards

I cautiously opened the door and looked outside

It seemed okay so I took a step onto the ground
"Argh!" I sank down into the warm, gooey stuff
The moon was made of porridge!

There were swirls of honey and sprinkles of sugar
And warm, milky porridge oats all around
Instead of having a slice of moon cheese
I spent my moon day swimming in porridge!

Will Saunders (10)
Glebe House School, Hunstanton

Flying On A Cat Adventure

Once in the garden
I was looking at the grass
Then I heard a meow
I didn't know what to do
So I went inside and had a stew
But I kept hearing it get louder and louder
So I followed the sound and it was at the beach
It looked black, hairy and big
I went to stroke it because it was lovely
But it was so excited to run after a stick
Then it came to me and put me on its back
We then flew up to the sky
It was amazing, we saw the Eiffel Tower
And the biggest tower I ever saw
But the best of all were the animals
And Disneyland!
I felt the clouds and heard the birds tweet
While the wind whooshed by
It was the most glorious trip ever

It was so cool that I could fly
It was really clever
How a cat I'd found on a street could fly.

Eliza Ann Dix (9)
Glebe House School, Hunstanton

Celebrations Tin

"Heave!" I shouted as all of us pushed
The Twix, the Galaxy and Bounty
All of us trying to escape the Celebrations tin
Of course, Bounty was at the bottom
Just like Tottenham
Snickers were shooting
While we were all pouncing as we stacked up
"One more heave!" I said
I was a Malteser
I was always teasing everyone
But this time, I was not teasing
One, two, three...
But before I could say 'heave'
The lid opened
I was clutched tightly
It was dark inside
I was squashed as I crunched
I heard a voice say, "Dear, oh dear."
Then I realised I was in a hand
And it moved, then let me go

As I shouted, "No!"
And into the bin I went
Where all the other wrappers went.

Annabel Lantos (10)
Glebe House School, Hunstanton

Cloud Shine

There once was a girl called Maisie
She always dreamed of having
An adventure on a cloud
One day, she woke up on a cloud!
She started off by having a nibble
Of the fluffy cloud. *Mmm!*
It tasted gummy, but
There was something in the distance
It was a... a... a plane!
Phew! I thought it would be something scary!
So she carried on playing
But she saw a man jumping on clouds
The man was walking to Maisie
He introduced himself
And he was called Bill
He seemed like a nice man
So Maisie made friends with him
They played and played, but the sun was rising
And then she woke up and realised
That it was all a wonderful dream.

Maisie March (10)
Glebe House School, Hunstanton

Recipe For A Friendship

I've often wondered about a recipe for friendship
With the perfect mix of love, it's a blend-ship
Sweetened generously with affection
Gives a deeper pal connection

Maybe a cup of faith
And two cups of kindness
Remember to season with politeness
Stir well then simmer gently
Feelings must be handled correctly
Garnish with some firm belief
To know you're loved is a happy relief

Good friends blend well and never part
Serve up beautiful, delicious memories
To keep warm in your heart

Now I've told you my warming recipe
Use it next time
All you need to do
Is follow the recipe!

Scarlett Holly Hallard (10)
Glebe House School, Hunstanton

Metamorphosis

I'm walking in the park
Jumping in the puddles
Splash! Splash! Splash! Bong!
What was that?

Antennae?
On my head?
Straight as sticks?
Long as limousines?

Wings? Pink and purple wings?
Round as circles?
Soft as pillows?

I'm shrinking!
Smaller than sweets?
Tall as a needle?
I'm tiny!

Antennae?
Wings?
Tiny?
I'm a butterfly!

Flying through flowers
Hearing their chit-chat
Tasting their nectar
Talking to them.

Soon, I'm back to normal
No antennae
No wings
Back to normal size!

Emelia King (10)
Glebe House School, Hunstanton

A Tea Party On A Cloud

A tea party on a cloud
Is peaceful, not loud
It seems upside down
But there's no need to frown
It is brilliant and fun
For everyone
We remembered to make
A delicious cake
We'll lay out the saucers for everyone
And we've baked cookies, which was fun
Clouds are full of fluff
It is very wet stuff
Now I'm writing in my diary
No one's attitude is fiery
Up here in the clear
Cold atmosphere
When we get back down
We start to frown
Because we miss being up high
In the clear, beautiful sky.

Orla Emily Haslam (10)
Glebe House School, Hunstanton

Colours Faded

As I doze off to sleep
My mind whirls with thoughts
Then I'm falling into an ocean
Splash!
The fish are swimming all around
I meet a clownfish
His white stripes are as white as snow
His orange stripes are as vibrant as mango
We swim in and out of the coral
As we go through the reef
It fades away
Slowly going white
"It's the pollution from the oil."
"The humans are killing our coral," says the fish
There's an alarm ringing in my head
I look everywhere for it
And I wake up.

Gracie-Mae Elizabeth Meek (10)
Glebe House School, Hunstanton

Pizza Dragon Party

P izza-loving dragon alive today
I ntelligent at making pizza
Z ootropolis-hater
Z ebra-mimicker
A nnoying to eat

D eadly pizzas galore
R ocket-lover
A nchovy-hater
G arlic bread eater
O nion-peeler
N ine pizzas at a time

P epperoni on top
A rancini as a starter
R umbling tummies galore
T ime for a muncher
Y ou and me, it's a delight!

Giovanni Giubileo (10)
Glebe House School, Hunstanton

Race Cars

The cars ripping up the track
More and more every lap
You hear them roaring as loud
As a tiger or a lion even
Cars racing after each other
Like a cheetah and a gazelle
Hundreds of miles an hour
Roar, roar as they go past
Driving as fast as a falcon
Last lap, "Winner! Winner!"
After the race, celebrate
Pouring champagne over each other
Screaming, "Argh!" Shouting with joy
Like a little boy with his race car toy.

Jonny Goode (10)
Glebe House School, Hunstanton

Making Tea On The Moon!

Making tea on the moon was very hard
For my teabags were all floating
I couldn't get my water into my kettle top
My mug wouldn't stay on the ground

So I had to compromise
I went to flick the gravity switch

But then I heard a crash, a smash and a clash
I found that I'd smashed my cup
Bashed my kettle
And my teabags were all over the place

In the end, I gave up and said
"Oh fine, I will just have a coffee!"

Edward Gostling (9)
Glebe House School, Hunstanton

Nature

One day, I went camping with Mummy and Alice
I saw lots of animals in the forest
I collected some wood for a warm fire
I felt happy camping, the owls hooted
Hedgehogs scurried around
We sat around the fire
I felt warm near the fire
I got into my tent to go to sleep
I lay awake in my pink sleeping bag
With Teddy on top
When I awoke, the sun shone yellow.

Emily Kilby (10)
Glebe House School, Hunstanton

The Song

The birds fly down
They sing so sweet
The trees dance
When the wind blows
The clouds rain down
When they cry

The birds fly down
They sing so sweet
They glide away
And dive down at prey
Smaller mother birds stomp and stir
To get them up and worms appear.

Ferdi Macewan (10)
Glebe House School, Hunstanton

A Picnic With A Mermaid

M aking sandwiches out of seashells
E ating seaweed cupcakes
R ock pool fun under the sun
M eeting mermaids, making friends
A ctually talking to a dolphin
I vy-coloured tail all covered in scales
D eep, blue sea and golden sand.

Philippa Hingley (7)
Glebe House School, Hunstanton

Ernie The Hoover

He's black and hairy
Just don't call him scary
He answers to Ernie
He's always hungry
And eats everything in sight
No bits are too big or too small
What's yours is his
He's very funny
Give him a treat
He'll answer to you.

Harry Jack John Hammond (9)
Glebe House School, Hunstanton

Imaginary World!

In my imaginary world, people eat candy
But at Christmas, you never have brandy
You can eat ice cream and just have dessert
The trees are L.O.L. dolls
The houses are rainbow mansions
You can even have tea with purrmaids and unicorns
But that's not all, the oceans are galaxy, glitter, sparkle sprinkles
Their poop is magic, but nothing is ever tragic
Because in Imaginary World, it's a happy world!
There's always world peace because
Everyone can wish for what they want.

Freya Whitlock (9)
Great Dunham Primary School, Great Dunham

My Week

I walked on Saturday
Until I fell out of the sky
I was eating a bag of sweets
And one fell in my eye

I danced on Sunday
Until I fell in a pot
Led away in a bubble that popped

I sprinted on Monday
Until I fell into a lava pit
I started to panic
Until I was saved by a rabbit

I jumped on Tuesday
Until I fell into the sea
I was drinking some cold water
Until a shark bit my knee

I talked on Wednesday
Until I fell off a cliff
I found myself in a jungle
And my legs became stiff

I swam on Thursday
Until I met a car
Rolling down a hill
Into a puddle of tar

I laughed on Friday
Until I met the balloon
Of the sea
This week has been full.

William Gardam (7)
Great Dunham Primary School, Great Dunham

My Sea Flea

I bought a house under the sea
What fascinating creatures would I see?
Some weird, some wonderful
Some out of this world
But the best of all was a flea

It swam like a muggle
It jumped in the air
It rumbled and tumbled
All over my chair

The food it smuggled
Was willing for a cuddle
Especially the fleas
Who loved a snuggle

My flea's my pet
My best pet
My most loving pet of them all

I love him
I love him
I hug him

I hug him
He's my flea under the sea!

Lyra Hill (9)
Great Dunham Primary School, Great Dunham

Fun In The Sun!

Summer is here, it's time to have some fun
As I walk to the beach, I see everyone
As I place down my sunbed
From miles away
I see a rainbow that looks far away
As I splash and splash in the waves
I suddenly fall into a cave
As I slowly look around
I see crabs, rubies, pearls and also fish
And in the corner, there is a jellyfish
That is pink
At the last second
I realise I am in a sink!

Gracie Garner (9)
Great Dunham Primary School, Great Dunham

The Sleepy Dragon

A dragon awoke in his mountain lair
Where he'd slept for a thousand years
His treasure was rusty, his scales were dusty
His throat was dry, his wings wouldn't fly
His fire was smoky, his eyes weren't flashing
HIs tail wasn't slashing, his claws couldn't scratch
Though he tried, he sighed
And stretched himself over the floor
And went back to sleep for a thousand years more.

Archie Cook (7)
Great Dunham Primary School, Great Dunham

My Weird But Wonderful Life

I got in a muddle, then fell in a puddle
When I got to the ground, I found
I was in a new land!
I thought I was in a daze
'Til the sky gave me a gaze
He said, "You are not
But you're covered in spots!"
I looked all around and I found the world
Was covered in dots and spots!
I found a cat and a bat, both in top hats!

Bella Hill (7)
Great Dunham Primary School, Great Dunham

Candy Land

One day in Candy Land
I woke up in a cloud of candyfloss
Then I had Fruit Loops for breakfast
After breakfast, I got dressed
When I was dressed, I went outside
And saw my friends at the park
I got some blueberry bubblegum
And then I blew a bubble
My friend popped it
And it started raining
But there was a lovely rainbow.

Holly Jessica Susan Appleby (7)
Great Dunham Primary School, Great Dunham

Sunbathe On Clouds

Summer in the sun gives loads of fun
With air on my face giving a sweet taste
From down below, I see a disco
With people dancing everywhere
With me up above and them down below
Shows me a sign of a rainbow
As I think of the rainbow colours
I remember my sisters and brothers
Suddenly, I see some people waving
My family!

Betha Chantry (9)
Great Dunham Primary School, Great Dunham

The Unicorn's Poop!

Unicorns' poop is rainbow and glittery
It is as beautiful as can be
Unicorns are lovely and so is their poop
Unicorns eat sprinkles and cupcakes
And that is what makes their poop a rainbow
Unicorns' hair is rainbow, like their poop
Unicorns' horns are rainbow too
Unicorns are the most magical creatures ever.

Esme Moxey (8)
Great Dunham Primary School, Great Dunham

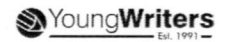

Max

A shark ate my sausage house
My dragon lit the fire
The jellyfish put it out
With a dash of light
A squid ate my snorkel
With a dash of salt
A troll ate my goggles
I pulled a face
And brushed my teeth with my dragon's toothbrush
But a squid stuck to my head
A fish swarm came and ate the seafloor.

Max Prochazka (8)
Great Dunham Primary School, Great Dunham

Unicorn Called Bee

Bea got invited to tea with a flea
She had a good time, her dinner was divine
She dropped her stuff in her basket
She got her fishing rod and cast it
She went to school and learned her topic
She saw a unicorn headband
And it was her top pick
She went home to bed and rested her head.

Jessica Wild (9)
Great Dunham Primary School, Great Dunham

The Amazing Adventure

I was walking when suddenly
I fell onto a candysaurus rex!
It took me to a land of candy dinosaurs
And to a den
I crawled inside
And I went swimming in a volcano
I swam and swam until I was home again.

Jamie White (7)
Great Dunham Primary School, Great Dunham

Invite An Elf To Tea

I invited an elf to tea
To have lots and lots of seaweed
He ate it all up
And walked off in a huff
I'll never invite him to tea again
I walked back home with a cloud of rain.

Isobel Clifton (9)
Great Dunham Primary School, Great Dunham

Stone Monster Dome

To survive Stone Monster Dome
You have to be a gnome
An alien tried but went and died
If you try, you might die
Can anyone survive Stone Monster Dome?

William Thomas Cooper (8)
Great Dunham Primary School, Great Dunham

Inside The Oak Tree

Inside the oak tree
Inside the oak tree
Guess what you can hear?
An opera ant singing
A monster that's digging
And a woodlouse having a ride!

Inside the oak tree
Inside the oak tree
Guess what you can see?
The butterflies fluttering by
A dragon singing a lullaby
And a ladybird playing in the snow!

Inside the oak tree
Inside the oak tree
Guess what you can feel?
The rough bark on the outside
The smooth wood on the inside
And the fresh water all over.

Laurence Redman (7)
Great Heath Academy, Mildenhall

My Food Galaxy

I live on Planet Cupcake
And it's the planet where we like to bake
My cousins live on Planet Burger
And love to eat Walkers crisps
My aunty lives on Planet Doughnut
And the planet loves nuts
My uncle lives on Planet Pizza
And really likes the pyramids of Giza
My friends live on Planet Gumball
And love going to balls
Any time I want to see them
I zoom away in my flying gummy bear
The stars show me the way.

Sola Akindiji (7)
Great Heath Academy, Mildenhall

Animals Of The Wild

Elephants' stomping feet and swirly trunks
Tigers' roaring jaws and pointy teeth
Looking to bite something
Zebras' clippity-cloppety hooves
And black and white stripes
Lions with their fluffy manes
Sitting on a rock with pride
They almost look tamed
Monkeys' cheeky, smiley faces
And their curly, swirly tails
Animals of the wild are such a sight to see.

Hayley Matzk (8)
Great Heath Academy, Mildenhall

What Is Wrong With Me?

The alien on my face
The octopus eating my sausage roll
The shark called Mark eating my banana
The fish eating my soggy mushroom
The bread is all mucky
A rabbit nibbling my toes
What is wrong with me?
Turtles bashing my nose
Swish, swish, swish
Boxes itching my back
My grandad laughing at me
What's wrong with me?

Clervi Kemp (8)
Great Heath Academy, Mildenhall

Crazy Unicorns

Unicorns have rainbow hair
They prance around without a care

Sparkly eyes that glitter
You cannot take your eyes off them

Unicorns like to play around
Sometimes, they leave the ground

Adventures through the woods,
Oh, how I would love to go!

Khloe Davidson (7)
Great Heath Academy, Mildenhall

Nature Adventure

Outside waits, it's out there for me
I'm the one for nature you see
A walk in the woods on a beautiful night
The moon gives me just enough light

Water rippling, trees rustling
On a busy day, it's oh so bustling
A damp petal lands on my cheek
Even better than growing a leek

Wolves howling, birds tweeting
Air billowing through my hair
The Tarzan of the forest
Land on a cloud

And float away...

Jaimee Andrews (9)
Hevingham Primary School, Hevingham

The Secret Lever!

I saw, on my way
To school one day
I saw a lever in the bush
That I just happened to push

It unlocked a magical world that day
I just decided to stay
It was so nice
It was like a slice
Of cake!

Marian Jane Sinclair-Russell (9)
Hevingham Primary School, Hevingham

A Loving Rose

Roses are red
Violets are blue
My girl is loving
And so are you

Snow is white
Ghosts are rare
Her voice is soft
And so is her hair

Magnolia grows
With bugs like eggs
Surfaces are smooth
And so are your legs

Sunflowers reach
Up to the skies
Stars are sparkling
And so are your eyes

Foxgloves in hedges
Surrounded the farms
A room is warm

And so are your arms

Daisies are pretty
Daffies have style
Flowers are beautiful
And so is your smile

A rose is beautiful
Just like you.

Maisey Reading (7)
Hockering CE (VC) Primary School, Hockering

For The Seasons I Want

For summer, I want
A hot barbecue
A spinning, disco dress
And candyfloss clouds

For spring, I want
Skipping lambs
Growing flowers
And the Easter Bunny

For winter, I want
Christmas with family
And to be buried in the snow

For autumn, I want
Black and orange outfits
And glowing pumpkins

For the seasons, I get
Flowers growing
Lambs skipping
Buried in the snow
And Christmas with my family.

Melody-Maye Birch-Rodney (7)
Hockering CE (VC) Primary School, Hockering

School

School
A boring, useless waste of time
It's not
A fun, happy place to go
Friends make it
Okay
Maths is fun
(Not)
I hate PE
Challenging
That's what I call Topic, I wish it was more fun
For beginners
IT is tough
An annoying, stinky prison
It's not a sunny blissful place
School

Once you've read my poem
Read it from the bottom to the top!

Tallulah Kati Goodwin (10)
Hockering CE (VC) Primary School, Hockering

Biscuits

I like biscuits
Any biscuit
Chocolate biscuits, custard creams
Biscuits in my biscuit dreams

Cheesy crackers, ginger nuts
Jammy Dodgers to cheer you up
Biscuits, yum, yum, yum
Biscuits in my tum!

Bourbon creams, Happy Faces
Biscuits in all sorts of different places
Home-made cookies (very nice)
Biscuits with some orange spice

I like biscuits
Any biscuit!

Dorothy Iwo (9)
Hockering CE (VC) Primary School, Hockering

Space Adventure!

I fly through the pitch-black sky
On an enchanted giraffe called Kai
Looking at planets that I want to own
Watching comets whizz and groan

On the planet of colours, I see purple cliffs
I'm pretty sure that they are just myths
Crystal lakes flow from a deep, dark cave
I like meals from microwaves

As I am thinking this, Kai is shouting
I look up. A giant, slithering snake
Comes through a rock at us but misses
What should we do? I think as it hisses

Fantastical beasts are just in stories
Maybe I am in a story or possibly a poem
I stare coldly at the slithering beast
And realise that I have to show him
That throwing rocks is not the way to go
And that is when he decides to go to my home in Morocco.

Chester Joscelyne (10)
St Helen's Primary School, Ipswich

Minor Magic

I teleport and see
A new land that's waiting for me!
As the creatures crawl, the world, they rule
As wonder fills their minds
Those people become blind
As the tree fills the sky
The wonders fly by
Out of their minds
They are free!
The more they think
The less they blink
Reading stories
Instead of making their own
They still do draw stories forever
And they do it together
Flying pinecones
All are mind-blown
Singing flowers
And unknown hours
Completely without inspiration
All it is is deformation

Then it is, it becomes midnight
The owls whistle and the stars twinkle
All people are sleeping
But one person's causing beeping
it is sunrise and the dolphins dive
Into the great, big sea
The monkeys are so cheesy
It is strange I think, but I don't take a blink
I ask the monkeys, "Why do you live by the ocean?"
They say, "It's only called motion."
A spectrum of blue and I slip with my stupid shoe
I enter a forest, I am scared
But only that minute do I realise
That only now it has become sunrise!
I fall into a dark, deep hole
I hope this isn't for a mole
I don't want to go back to my world
So I sit here, curled.

Viktorija Gerlikaite (10)
St Helen's Primary School, Ipswich

Into Your Nightmares

The day all trees fell
People dropped like flies
Revolutionary-red blood oozing
From their peppered bodies
But from a nightmare, this lies
On this page, it pulls tears, terrors and traumas
However, all is a segment from one adult's dreams

Running and running
But not fast enough
Monsters creeping behind
Stepping on one's shadow
Pulling on their food consumers
But from a nightmare, this lies
On this page, it cuts, curses and creeps
However, all is an aspect from one teenager's fears.

Cloning once
Again, again and once again
Never-ending machinery, compelling minds
To agree and never misplace similarity

But from your nightmare, this lies
On this page, it freezes fear, fighting and force
However, all is a piece from one child's (sometimes) unfriendly imagination

Beside all happiness, these sit
From your nightmares, these lie
It shouldn't, it should be unicorns
And dreams of one as a future footballer, artist, dancer
But from your nightmares, it does
And so it shall be
Nightmares: the horrific things that haunt you in the dark.

Bonnie Elvin (10)
St Helen's Primary School, Ipswich

The Wacky Pollution Place

Down in the depths of the ocean
Fish have been radiated
Now they can speak and are gradually growing legs
Slowly yet surely becoming more intelligent
So come to the Wacky Pollution Palace today
Let the methane control your body!
Cleanse yourself in radiation and diesel
You want change?
Go to the radiation sauna
You want stink bombs?
Trump into a bottle and donate it to us!
After all, it's methane!

The owner, Mr Pufferfish, loves methane
He grabs it by the hand, he pulls it in
It holds the best value
It holds the best smell
It doesn't hold as much pollution
Which is good for the environment
As much as it is for you!

A creepy customer (a horrid human)
Did not agree with this place
So now they are fundraising
Here and there
To stop this place from polluting
They are trying to obtain our diesel
Radiation, petrol and all
You guessed it
Even the methane!

Now Mr Pufferfish shuns the humans
So you are definitely lucky
For you are not human
Wait, you are a human?
Forget what I just said...

Callum Matthew Papworth (11)
St Helen's Primary School, Ipswich

The Boy Without A Clue Taking A Bath

Up, up
And up once more
A tub of soapy water lay upon a mountain
Within which a clueless boy was inserted
The clouds passed his porcelain bath by the thousands
As he washed himself in bubbles and ignorance

Down from here
Down, down some more
A town of scholars bustled at the foot of the mountain
Eager students grinning in every school
Facts phasing into their already knowledgeful minds by the hundreds
As they learnt with excitement and wonder

The townsfolk wanted to help the boy
They tried, they really did!
Offering him literature of Dickens and Bronte
But the simple 'Ugly Duckling', he shunned with disgust

Encouraging a non-existent spark of creativity
By showing him Mozart and Van Gogh
When 'Twinkle, Twinkle, Little Star' left a puzzled expression

So from then on
(We're talking to the end of eternity)
Our boy sat in his soapy tub on the peak of the mountain
His head which within nothing was inserted
The world proceeding in intelligence below him
As he washed in bubbles and ignorance.

Ollie Joseph (11)
St Helen's Primary School, Ipswich

Phantasmagorical Dream

What was this world I could see?
This was a whole world of fantasy!
With the rainbows up in the sky,
Majestic and mythical creatures flew by!
Suddenly, purple aliens came out, floating in the air,
I was so surprised, completely unaware!
For whatever reason, they started to prance like animals,
Who would've thought me and an alien were compatible?
When we stopped dancing and our party had ended,
I felt like we were really connected!
After that, I decided to go and explore this wonderful land
So I flew over to the palace door,
But then I noticed there was something wrong with the floor!
"Argh!" I screamed as I got sucked into a bright blue portal!
Wake up! Wake up! I heard in my head,

I woke up and saw I was in my violet bed!
I also saw my family surrounding me,
Telling me that I was having a dream!
It couldn't be, could it? But it was so real!
I came to the conclusion that it was all a phantasmagorical dream.

Asal Azhdari (10)
St Helen's Primary School, Ipswich

Books Full Of Morals

There are books, books, books everywhere
With pages that are the shade of the stony ground
Grabbing you like tentacles
The ink thrown across each line imaginatively
So, I read them... My eyes scan, searching for meaning
North, south, east, west
Somehow, in my mind, I can hear the books talking
Telling me about stories inside their hearts
Stories from pirates and fairies to non-fiction books
Where facts about magnets and maiasaura dance
Sometimes, there are morals that are a rule book about how to live our lives
Triumphantly, this compendium of books flies
Through forests, oceans, African plains and haunted castles
Somebody who never reads is walking across a street
His eyes are dim; his ears haven't heard the sweetness
Of the words in stories

Soon, books wrap around him, encouraging him to read
Now this boy always reads; his mind is alive
His ears hear forests of sounds... he is found.

Jonah George Merchant (10)
St Helen's Primary School, Ipswich

Crazy Dreams

In my bedroom, where I stayed put
My mind went blank and my imagination sank
Tired eyes closed shut
But a crab appeared and baked some pies!
"What is this nonsense?" I asked Mr Crab
"I don't know," he said. "Just grab."

A black hole appeared and made me sink
And then I heard a chick
The chick I heard made me go onto a brink
Creatures took me to an underwater barbecue
And they made me sink
My worries flew by and made me fly
Into a world of creatures nearby.

This adventure was really fun
But ended with a pun!
"Oh no!" I screamed
This day was not for me!
I opened my eyes
And there I flew into my bed with a stew.

Everything was gone

Creatures and animals
But it was time to start my day
And go back to my stack of hay!
At the end of the day, Santa Claus came!

Amelia Grzesiak (10)
St Helen's Primary School, Ipswich

Why I Am Different With Autism

I am different but the same as you,
But why do I need to do things I don't want to?
Like going to the park
Or playing football.
My tablet is my fun with games and videos to learn from.
It's not my fault that I like things that remove me from society.
I find it hard to control my feelings.
I try to keep them down when I am at school
Because I worry that I will get into trouble.
But at home, I shout and scream and cry,
Noise in the classroom can be
Irritating,
Distracting,
But okay when it benefits the lesson.
At playtime, I like to be on my own with my leaves and sticks.
I'm not sad,
I'm happy all alone,

But sometimes, I do get lonely
Watching children play,
But the games they play
Sometimes break the rules,
So I stay away.
This is my life with autism.

Nathan Watson (8)
St Helen's Primary School, Ipswich

Up My Chimney

Now, some girls went down a rabbit hole
I went up my chimney
Whoosh! Up and up, past the grubby soot, I flew
How did this happen? Where am I going?
Who will be up there with me?
I closed my eyes just as I shot out
I started to see what was up here
Cotton candy, lots of sugary treats
To eat very greedily
Along with all those sweets
There was also a very cute, pink gummy dog
What could I see next? Anything!
But what I saw was the last thing anyone would expect
A unicorn dancing ballet very crazily
What an amazing wonderland
But I didn't see that my chimney was fading
"Argh!" I ran home, well, to my chimney
I wanted my mum, I wanted my home
I wanted my dad and all my family

Now, when you get home
Have a little look up your chimney!

Scarlett Borrett (9)
St Helen's Primary School, Ipswich

Alien In My Room

In my bedroom, lying down
Then suddenly, I was gone
"What is this?" I asked myself
I was with an alien named John

He said that I'd been chosen
But I didn't know what to say
He wanted me to go with him
So I said, "Go away."

He looked like he had tentacles
And ten googly eyes
His mouth was blue
And full of fries

He grabbed my hand and I went *whoosh!*
Into an imaginary world
Where I could see all kinds of things
Especially things that curled

Then I saw something that caught my eye
It was as crazy as could be
It was a town made out of peas!

Evie Armstrong (10)
St Helen's Primary School, Ipswich

Creatures In Space

I sat in my parents' car
It started with no driver
Speeding off a cliff, it seemed like a myth
Not going down, but up, up, up
Into space
I looked back at Earth
Then on Saturn
I saw a unicorn surf!
A boy sat on the moon toasting marshmallows on a fire!
To go to space was always something I would desire
Still in my parents' car from Earth
I was so far
Even though the sun was so hot
An alien sat on top
The car started to wiggle and jiggle
Then I noticed a colossal squid attached to the car
It didn't seem so dangerous for it fired the car
The car reversed and went back to my home on Earth.

Nicholas Mikov (10)
St Helen's Primary School, Ipswich

Dragons Will Rule The Future

Dragons will rule in the future
I am very sure of that
Dragons will rule in the future
And they will be very fat
Dragons will rule
And they will be cruel
Dragons will rule in the future
If they don't, they will rule a pool
Dragons will rule in the future
And make a magical world
My prediction is weird and wonderful
Even though it is dangerous
Dragons will rule in the future
And we will be left on an island far from land
And sleep in a cave that once belonged to
A dragon who was hugely fat!

Alfred Catherall (10)
St Helen's Primary School, Ipswich

The Plan Of The Future

This is the future
Dragons grin to win
They could be extremely thin
Like a harlequin
Saturn has turned into a cookie
Why? Well, nobody knows, such a pity!
Mushrooms with a duvet of dust?
Well, the dragon has disappeared with a poof of trust
Blobfish has run for president
Blobfish has also won
This is the future
How do we survive?
Grin? No, we aren't dragons!
The answer is... there is no answer
But what we do know is
The cookie must've belonged to a blob
Wait... what?

Emily Yeung (10)
St Helen's Primary School, Ipswich

Petrifying Volcanoes - Be Aware!

Not
Like before
I took away
My greatest fears
And faced the colossal monster
No one knew what I was doing
But I had a great, smart plan
It was an erupting volcano squirting lava
The smoke billowing out like clouds before it rains
I had to save our city
I had to save the entire world!
I saw a ginormous boulder bigger than a car
And then I did it, definitely now, not later
I threw the boulder on top of the volcano's hot lava
"I've saved the amazing, mighty world!"

Esme Ellen Merchant (8)
St Helen's Primary School, Ipswich

A Kind Girl With A Kind Heart

In a town not far away
There is a girl enjoying her day
She is very kind and never rude
If you see her, she'll be coming up to you
If she does, she will say
"Hey, how are you doing today?
Then she will leave to leave you alone
This girl talks without having to moan
If you dare to be mean
The police put you in a cellar
If you don't know who this girl is
Her name is Cinderella
I don't know why, but this is true
Otherwise, you may have ended up
In a cage from the zoo!

Tahiya Afsana Hye (9)
St Helen's Primary School, Ipswich

My Baby Pet Dragon

I woke up not in my bedroom
But with a dragon in front of me!
It was a cute, purple, soft and shiny one
And it called me Mama instead of my name!

I looked after it for a few years
And it grew up big and strong
It drank from the Goblet of Fire
And I taught it how to fly!

One day, I rode on its back
And I saw the whole Milky Way!
But suddenly, I slipped and fell off its back
And found out it was just a dream.

Yosr Al Hassan (11)
St Helen's Primary School, Ipswich

The Next Dodo?

Everything you use
Everything you eat
All has palm oil in
Because it is cheap

But not to me, it is very rare
Because people use it everywhere

But what I'm talking to you about
Is orangutans with no doubt
They lose their homes every day
And it leaves them with nowhere to play

So next time you go to the shops
Check the ingredients to see what you've got.

Tess Thompson (9)
St Helen's Primary School, Ipswich

I Apologise For My Appetite

I apologise for my appetite
for my breakfast was divine,
I apologise for my appetite
for my lunch was delicious,
I apologise for my appetite
for my dinner was magnificent,
I apologise for my appetite
for my supper was fantastic,
I apologise for my appetite
but I am not fat!

Alfie Weston (10)
St Helen's Primary School, Ipswich

It's Raining Bananas, Mushrooms And Keys

Wow, it's raining bananas
What a wonderful sight
What a delight

Wow, it's raining mushrooms
What an amazing sight
What a big, fun time
What a delight

Wow, it's raining keys
What a lovely sight
What a delight
Wow, it's raining bananas.

Cooper Flurrie (7)
St Helen's Primary School, Ipswich

Weird Things

Aliens with burger guns
A whole lot of nonsense
What is this?
There is more!
Someone with noodle arms
His name is Joe
He is normal, but his arms
Are the odd ones out!
And there's also talking spaghetti.

Malik Nour (7)
St Helen's Primary School, Ipswich

Magical Wardrobe

I went to my bedroom, I heard banging and cracking
I looked around but could see nothing
I opened my eyes and what I saw
Was a magical wardrobe just in front of me
The noise was getting loud
I was worried a little bit
Who was hiding inside, what kind of freak?
Then the door opened and I stood still
Unicorns, mermaids, elves, trolls and more
Popped out of the closet without a second thought
I'm dreaming? No kidding, I'm spinning! What's happening?
They were playing, they were jumping
They were everywhere now!
"Stop! Leave! I want you all out!
Who are you? Who are you?
The game is over now!"
I screamed and I screamed
Then I woke up
The magical wardrobe was gone!

Olivia Ali (7)
St Margaret's Primary Academy, Lowestoft

Elephant Tea Party

Oh yes, the elephants are here!
I am so excited, everyone cheer!
They all sit down and they all have a crown
For they're the best elephants in town
I ask what they want and they say, "Nuts!"
"Oh, okay."
I get some nuts and they all have a smile
And you can see it for a mile
It is all going so well until...

All the nuts are gone and taken
My masterpiece cake has disappeared
Where has it all gone?
Will we ever get a tea party that won't go wrong?
Elephant God, save us in our misery
All the food is gone and now it's not a tea party anymore
All the goodies are gone
Our glory is no more
And me and the elephants have been put in boredom and hunger.

Tess Smith (10)
St Margaret's Primary Academy, Lowestoft

Our Lovely Teacher, Mrs Kennedy

Our lovely teacher, Miss Kennedy
Is one I've never had before
Our lovely teacher, Miss Kennedy
Is as lovely as a flower
Who is kind and sweet every day
She has beautiful, yellow hair
With a sweet, blue dress
To add some fashion to this mess
Our lovely teacher, Miss Kennedy
Is very sweet at heart
She is an independent woman
And is always great
But she can be scary when she's really angry
Our lovely teacher, Miss Kennedy
She is one of the best
I will never forget
Our lovely teacher, Miss Kennedy
Is the star of the class
And I hope she is with us forever.

Jodi-Mae Leaper (9)
St Margaret's Primary Academy, Lowestoft

Tea In The Sea

I found at my door
Something I'd never seen before
An invitation to tea
With a shark under the sea!

I was first thinking it was a joke
And was really quite amused
But after a short while
I was so confused!

I found a swimming costume
And dived into the water
Soon I was sipping tea
With a shark under the sea!

When we had to say goodbye
It wasn't very nice
I got back onto the sand
But I was as cold as ice!

I was wrapped up in a blanket
And one thing is for sure
I won't forget my tea in the sea!

Lilli Smith-Cushion (9)
St Margaret's Primary Academy, Lowestoft

Raining Tacos

One morning, I woke up,
I got out of my bed,
I looked out of the window
And thought I was out of my head.

It was raining tacos!
No, that can't be right.
It had been raining tacos
For half the night!

I looked at the washing line,
Oh no! I looked at my party dress,
It was an astonishing mess!

My party was this afternoon.
Would my dad get it washed so soon?

Well, at least I'd get a free lunch,
It was time to go and have a munch!

Imogen Louise Lungenmuss-Ward (9)
St Margaret's Primary Academy, Lowestoft

A Monster With Me!

A monster and me
We met a bee
We are always friends
And we make trends
We love all
And all love us
When we do barbecues
The monster lights it up
It's up in the stars
Where he lives
He loves it
And I do also
If we meet again
I want to thank you
You're the best in the world
I'm the boy who likes you
You'll be in my heart
For all of that is true.

Taio Xavier Dyer (8)
St Margaret's Primary Academy, Lowestoft

My Trip To School On The Bouncing Road

All the roads are made of trampolines
And all the cars are bouncing along
We are bouncing high and I can see really far
I am thirsty, but I don't want to spill my drink in the car
This makes my trip to school really fun
It makes my tummy feel like it's upside down
When our trip is done, I feel a little sad
But I'm happy knowing that after school
I will be back in the car with my dad.

Gracey Leitch (7)
St Margaret's Primary Academy, Lowestoft

The Penguin Who Got Lost In Space!

Oh no! I'm lost
Lost where?
Lost in space!
My rocket ship left me
How I do not know
But I really miss the snow

All I hear is the crackling on Mars
And the twinkling stars
I look around the bright, shining moon
And I see another penguin
Staring back at me!

We decide to sit
And have a nice cup of tea
Why? Because we're stuck on the moon!

Connor-Joe Reeve (8)
St Margaret's Primary Academy, Lowestoft

The Lucky Leprechaun

He fills me with money and love
He can be lucky, like me, and sad
But he is magical like fairies
And I like magic
He gives me a coin to spend on love
Love is what I need to have
And you don't have to be rich
You need luck and love, like me
I've got love and luck
And that fills me with happiness
But there is love in everyone
Because you all love someone.

Malaja White (7)
St Margaret's Primary Academy, Lowestoft

A Dragonette's Life

A little creature
In a cave somewhere
Spread its wings into the air
The little creature was a dragon
Who got taken away in a wagon
His mother dear
Was killed by a spear
And that left the dragonette an orphan
The wagon stopped outside our mansion
And the dragon flew to our window
We looked after it for evermore
The little dragon was an orphan no more.

Kaitlyn Rihanna (9)
St Margaret's Primary Academy, Lowestoft

The Plague

Have you heard about the plague?
It makes you very beige
You don't want to catch it
You could catch it from fleas and nits
Do you want to feel the pain?
It makes you go insane
Who is to blame for getting the plague?
The pain is so intense
You can feel the sense
It makes you very drowsy and sick
But who is to blame for getting the plague?

Brayden Finnigan
St Margaret's Primary Academy, Lowestoft

Unicorn

I believe in unicorns, I do, I do, I do
People say they're not real
But I believe they're true

Magical and enchanted
Mythical creatures
I wish I could reach out
And touch them

Beautifully flowing hair
Which makes people stop and stare
I believe in unicorns, I do, I do, I do.

Lexie-Mai Finnigan (7)
St Margaret's Primary Academy, Lowestoft

I Am A Unicorn

I am a unicorn with soft, fluffy fur
My friend is a dragon and a catdog
I play all day and night with my magic
I wake up, stretch my hooves
Wake my friends up for a magic play
But Catdog is gone
Everyone is worried
And scared for him
Eventually, we find him
So we play for the day
It is so fun!

Ava Cregan (7)
St Margaret's Primary Academy, Lowestoft

The Magic BBQ

The dragon set fire to the underwater barbecue
For the unicorn and mermaid too

They made lots of nice things to drink and to eat
They even invited me

Little did I know that it was a magic barbecue
So it went so quickly
The mermaid said
"Have a sweet."
So I had a lick.

Ellie Davies (8)
St Margaret's Primary Academy, Lowestoft

Magical Unicorn School

I am a unicorn on my first day of school
But I must stop and put on my uniform
So I can be cool

There is a magical shop on my way there
Just a skip and a hop
And I hope the weather is fair

The school is high up in the clouds
I fly to meet my friend in a crowd.

Imogen Ardley (7)
St Margaret's Primary Academy, Lowestoft

Sweetie World

Some houses are made of chocolate cake
And some are made out of chocolate orange cake.
The swimming pools are made of bear sweets
And the clouds are made of marshmallows.
Rainbows are made out of Fruit Pastilles
And the sky is blueberry slush,
What a sweet world that will be!

Liam Coote (7)
St Margaret's Primary Academy, Lowestoft

Candy Cane Friend

This is my little candy cane friend
He likes to go on runs
He does almost everything
But he can't play the drums
Then one day, he falls off a tree
And the little candy cane friend cries
'Cause when January comes around
The little candy cane friend will die!

Megan Hammond (9)
St Margaret's Primary Academy, Lowestoft

Celebration Time

Here we go. I don't know
Can I do this?
Can I make it?
There is no reason why
I wouldn't take it.

Come on, come on
There is no way
How insane is this?
Are you going out of your mind?
My mind is blown!
I guess it's celebration time!

Adi Shuckford (10)
St Margaret's Primary Academy, Lowestoft

Flying Sandwiches

Roses hang from my feet
As the sandwiches that I eat
Go into a world of wonder
Castles as tall as skyscrapers
And tea parties on the moon
I see a mushroom village
But it's time to go
So let's get into my spaceship
And fly to the world below.

Serena Summer Ruby Goulbourne (9)
St Margaret's Primary Academy, Lowestoft

Crazy Ways

I'm sunbathing on a cloud
And the unicorns are very loud
I'm in a fairy tale
And I've met some whales

I'm in a gingerbread house
And I'm eating it
I'm having lots of fun
And there are lots of crazy ways!

Savannah Georgina Gail Wild (8)
St Margaret's Primary Academy, Lowestoft

Colours Of The World

The grass is green
The sky is blue
Apples are red
Clouds are white
The ocean is blue
Water is clear
Trees are brown
Those are the colours of the world
And the colours of the rainbow
You should like them too.

Eve-Louise Chapman (8)
St Margaret's Primary Academy, Lowestoft

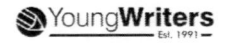

Unicorn

Unicorns are so cute
And they are so cuddly
They are so beautiful
So that's why people like them
They have lots of fluff
Unicorns are really, really good
I wish you could take one home as a pet.

Mary-Jane Joyce Gammage (8)
St Margaret's Primary Academy, Lowestoft

Liam's Awesome Cool Poem

There once was a boy from France
Who sometimes liked to dance
He liked to tap
And liked to clap
But his favourite thing was to prance.

Liam Gee (9)
St Margaret's Primary Academy, Lowestoft

Donkey Dance

There once was a donkey from France
Who really hated to dance
He did the floss
And got cross
So he did the super-duper dance!

Aidan Green (9)
St Margaret's Primary Academy, Lowestoft

Young Writers Information

We hope you have enjoyed reading this book – and that you will continue to in the coming years.

If you're a young writer who enjoys reading and creative writing, or the parent of an enthusiastic poet or story writer, do visit our website **www.youngwriters.co.uk**. Here you will find free competitions, workshops and games, as well as recommended reads, a poetry glossary and our blog. There's lots to keep budding writers motivated to write!

If you would like to order further copies of this book, or any of our other titles, then please give us a call or visit **www.youngwriters.co.uk**.

Young Writers
Remus House
Coltsfoot Drive
Peterborough
PE2 9BF
(01733) 890066
info@youngwriters.co.uk

Join in the conversation!
Tips, news, giveaways and much more!

YoungWritersUK   **@YoungWritersCW**